Planting the Voice

University of Central Florida
Contemporary Poetry Series

Planting the Voice

POEMS FROM POEMS

Lynn Butler

UNIVERSITY OF CENTRAL FLORIDA PRESS

ORLANDO

Library of Congress Cataloging-in-Publication Data

Butler, Lynn, 1945–
    Planting the voice : poems from poems / Lynn Butler.
        p. cm—(University of Central Florida contemporary poetry series)
    ISBN 0-8130-0921-9 (cloth)/(alk. paper)
    ISBN 0-8130-0937-5 (paper)
    I. Title. II. Series.
PS3552.U82624P5 1989
811'.54—dc19   88-32407
                                                  CIP

University Presses of Florida is the central agency for scholarly publishing of the
State of Florida's university system, producing books selected for publication by
the faculty editorial committees of Florida's nine public universities. Orders for
books published by all member presses should be addressed to University
Presses of Florida, 15 NW 15th Street, Gainesville, Florida 32603.

Acknowledgments

Grateful acknowledgment is made to the following publications in which my poems have appeared:

"Lacking the Words, the Vision" in *The Crescent Review* 2 (Fall 1984)

"For Maurice Utrillo" in *The Florida Review* 12 (Winter 1984)

"The Warrior Goddess in Her Elements" and "Glykera Leaves the School of Sappho" in *Kalliope* 2 (Winter 1980)

"Josefina Manresa Admonishes Her Fiancé" in *The Raddle Moon* (October 1984)

FOR JERRY SCHIFFHORST

animae dimidium meae

Contents

THE VOICES OF TIME

SACRED AND PROFANE SECRETS: THE BRONTË POEMS

*Poems from poems, songs
from songs, paintings from paintings,
always this friendly
impregnation.*

Adam Zagajewski, *"A River"*

*For an artist . . . the choice of epigraphs equals a declaration
of intention, a guide to reading and comprehension, allowing
us to see the new work in the light of past works, whose
memory it has kept and to which it feels a need to
respond. . . . The quotation is a viaticum on the threshold of a
journey that faces unexplored lands, the space of night, the
places of disunion.*

Jean Starobinski, *"Poetry between Two Worlds"*

To Catch the Song

Home

Le noyé cherche la chanson
*Ou s'était formé son jeune age. . . .**
Jules Supervielle

To catch the song!
That's why I want to go back.

I love it. I have always loved it.
More than my mother, more than my friends.

I long for this song in its purest vowels.
That's why I want to go back!

The original singers may all be gone
but even their absence will brim with song.

*The drowned man searches for the song in
which his youth was formed.

Invitation

For Edith Boissonnas

Come! My mind has breasts as soft
as my body's, a neck that unfolds for
the traffic of angels, a tail as bold
as the Carabas cat's, an eighteenth-
century spine. There are streams
in my mind, shade trees and clouds
in the wandering valleys that bring us
relaxing rain. There are steeply pitched
roofs with storks on the chimneys over
crooked, shadowed streets where the bells
of St. Ouen and the bell of the muffin
man brighten the evening. In the pie-
shaped room that is under the attic
your bed is covered with quilts and
pillows. There is snow at the window,
a candle to read by, a gold-rimmed
porcelain pot for chocolate. Outside
the village is a path through the
willows and a narrow wooden bridge
that leads to treasured Chenonceaux.
And far to the south you may see on the
mountain La Grande Chartreuse, whose
beauty can never show its face to you.

The Carabas cat is Perrault's Puss 'n Boots.

Where Do You Get Your Subjects?

For Amir Gilboa

Sometimes a line will settle itself
on the branch of a tree
and smile like the Cheshire cat.

And sometimes a tear
that I shed in 1960
will fall in my hand from a cloud.

And then a ray of sunlight
may lie right down before me,
portentous as an effigy.

Then again,
a blast of something enormous
will call out my name.

March 1983

For Maurice Utrillo

The light came,
damp, neglected,
looking for Utrillo.
She wasn't the full-grown
light of summer,
that dancer of the Air Cafe
whose act was followed by Monet,
but a child light, a March light,
a hushed light, a muteness
of shutters and snow.
All the young painters
held out their art
to cheer her, to warm her,
to dye her face with cosmetics,
to dress her up like a doll.
She twisted away,
running down side streets,
pausing in doorways
of churches and factories,
wineshops, bakeries,
crying for Utrillo,
"Papa! Papa!"

Lacking the Words, the Vision

I keep looking in poem
after poem. I never find it.
Only you, Tadeusz Rozewicz,
make an effort to see it.
But I, I have no son or daughter.
I am not the mother-in-law
you praise, that old foot-soldier
in the war against disorder.
I know I am a retired teacher,
the ex-ex-wife of a deceased
ex-husband, an amateur painter,
a woman who watches sunsets
and coupons, who naps and who dreams

she is a young girl, a silly girl,
the favorite daughter of indulgent
parents, budding, irresistible.
And around me hovers the aged
Goethe, drunk on the smell
of my soul and body,
dreaming his dream of me.
But nothing comes of all this.
If I could know. . . .
I do know. I must be something
more. I am something more.
But what? Why—
Why won't you poets tell me?

Fernando Pessoa Enters America

Jobs are circling him
with wild red eyes
and electric commandments
are prodding him on:
Go out, go out,
take up some duties
and get things done
Hurry! Hurry!
time is awasting
and time is money
what have you earned
in the past two weeks
whatever it is
you can earn much more
if you do as we tell you
here is some money
Good! you're listening
here is some money
all of it's yours
except for the taxes
here is your money
now give us your time
and don't tell us

Time is my body

here is some money
now give us some time
ah, that's how we do it
just open a little
why that didn't hurt
now that's how you do it
and now you're a man

Circle

Li hoje quase duas paginas
*Do livro dum poeta mistico**
Fernando Pessoa

So he borrowed
some flowers and stones and rivers.
That isn't so bad.
By your own admission
the flowers don't care
that a mystic used them,
the stones aren't lying there
feeling abused,
and the unblocked rivers go on and on and on
just as before.

Only you are disturbed ·
by a useless action:
invoking flowers and rivers and stones
and trying to blow some feeling
into them, or pretending
you have blown feeling into them,
that just like a spirit,
they weep and sweat.

Let's not be annoyed
by impossible efforts.
He gave you a laugh
and that isn't so bad, is it?
and he—San Juan, Fray Luis,
Senhor de Guimaraens—
gave me a ride on the flight
of his poems, those poems
that rise up like birds, like bread,
like steam, like sex, like mystical poets.

*I read today two pages in a book by a mystical
poet.

9

St. John of the Cross,
Remembering the Fever Hospital, Consults St. Teresa

"Some say that suffering
is a needle of the devil.

Others call it a pearl
rolled from the treasure of God.

Which do you say it is, *mi madre?*"

"The sufferings of others
are letters cut in the flesh of our breasts.

If there is light
in back of these letters,

its brilliance eclipses the words.

If there is darkness,
it is blacker than the new moon

and impossible to see by.

Now our own pain is
a *reloj de sol.*

Neither God nor the devil
can push its hands.

Day after day it is filed by the wind,
but no man in his life can say,

'I see the difference that the wind has made,'
without lying."

Reloj de sol: sundial.

Technē

For Louise Bogan

1

I wanted Apollo
but refused instead.
I dreaded the thrust
of his sun-hot shaft
ploughing the tones
in my head.
So now I am not
a harvest of music
I might have said.
My head is a pasture
of flowering sounds,
a weedy bed.

2

I wanted Apollo;
you came instead.
I flinched at the claim
of his loaded flesh
pointing its aims
at my head.
So now I am not
the captive of music
I might have said.
It was my body
bore your goal.
My head is the hostess
of passing sounds,
a childless soul.

Technē: art or skill.

Starry Night

For Violeta Parra

One night I heard
an odd little song
singing: Men had found out
that rape was all wrong.
So I straddled the curb
and lifted my dress,
shouting, "Well? Well?"
just to give it a test.
And all of the men
came flocking around,
"That's the prettiest
vulva, ma'm, in town.
Allow us to wish it
all of the best."
Then I jumped to my feet,
and sang to the stars,
chased down all streets,
got drunk in all bars,
made light of the dark
and danced on the sea,
cartwheeled the park,
fell asleep in a tree.

Winter Questions

What are the dead doing?

Moving invisible lips to shape invisible
prayers and parting invisible reeds with
hems of invisible robes while crossing
invisible streams that water invisible
fields to get to invisible shrines under
invisible oak trees.

O God, is all this what You wanted?

Couldn't the dead just sit and hold us?

Poetry

For Marina Tsvetaeva

You who are the soul of words
come and go inside them, Clear One.
I know when You visit my mouth and paper.

I know when You are absent,
although I still make shadowy marks
on the page in front of me.

Whatever I write without You
has nothing of life,
no power of flight or singing.

Look on these marks as rinds and breadcrumbs
dropped to attract You,
to draw You down to my mind and spirit.

Alight on this finger, Paraclete.

Simchat Sirah

I am a shtetl Jewess.
I trade in poems.
I finger each one
that comes to my counter.
I test its gold.

I stay on my street
for year after year
while others adventure.
They tell me their stories.

I tell them my joy:
the six-winged car
of Judah Halevi, of Uri Zvi Greenburg
brings me the Ages,
brings me Jerusalem.

Day after day
I get up at dawn
to put out my treasures,
some for the purse
of each heart.

My face and my eyes
are aging, but—
I sleep in the back of my shop,
I eat with my poems,
I keep Shabbas in the midst of them.

Simchat Sirah: Joy of the Song (or Poem).

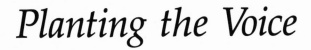

Planting the Voice

Cutting

For Jorge Carerra Andrade

When I read "isla de soledades y campanas," "isla
   de soledades,"
I longed to break off, perfectly,
that line from your lines,
and plant it in my soul,
watch it take root, throw out its shoots,
and flower,
         and discover how we,
in spite of our countries, our ages,
are closer than sister and brother,
are the same earth, the same mother.

Isla de soledades y companas: island of solitudes and bells.

Amnon and Thamar

y vió en la luna los pechos
*durísimos de su hermana**

So you, Amnon,
saw your own breasts

in the spotted moon
and called them, My sister,

saw your own hollow
in clefts of trees

and your long stolen hair
in the undulating rushes.

So, of course, Amnon,
when the body of Thamar

in the nakedness of water
and the globed enticement of the peony

freshened the night,
your flat, fevered body

breathed out a scirocco.

Now it is not a flower
that roots in her eyes.

*And he saw in the moon the hard breasts of his
sister.

Forever, Thamar
will see in the lightning

the play of a powerful sword
and an old tree

in the trunk of your sex, Amnon,
hollow and rotten.

Preciosa La Vieja Enseña Al Aire

A Clitoral Hymn

*Abre en mis dedos antiguos
la rosa azul de tu vientre**

She is not
in my womb,
the blue rose
of my womb.
This blue-
blooded rose
is the star
of my portal.

Rose of my midnight,
rose of my dawning,
rose of my romance,
rose of my madness.

O rose,
blue as the sea,
your sister immortal,
rising and falling
like tides and
churned by the
turning moon.
What goddess
invented you,
rose, rose?
Blooming even
as I wither,
powerful
in my frail body.

Title: Preciosa the Old Lady Teaches the Wind.

*Open to my old fingers the blue rose of your womb.

The Martyrdom of Eulalia

Su sexo tiembla enredado
*como un pájaro en las zarzas**

It is a bird
trying to walk,
not to fly this morning.
(Such power
is not even dreamed of.)

It is a bird
trailing her wings,
trying to steady
her balance.

It is a bird. . . .

But who crushed her?
Who dropped on her
the stone of his passion?

*Her sex trembles surrounded
like a bird in the underbrush.

Sisters 1825

Por las ramas del laurel
vi dos palomas desnudas.
La una era la sol,
la otra la luna. *

A pair of dark doves
flew over Haworth.
One dove was the sun;
one dove was the moon.
They sang to three sisters,
"Life will be old soon,
Death will be young soon."

Emilia was swift.
With a blow of her foot
She stamped down her roots
deep where she stood.
"I will stay where my heart
can bear its wild flower."

Carlota was slower.
The strings of her heart
sent forth its *saetas*
of dolorous women.
These were her offspring.
The false child would kill her.

The shadow of doves
fell black upon Ana.

*Through the branches of laurel I saw
two dark doves. One was the sun,
one was the moon.

Saetas: arrows, piercing songs.

She heard in their song,
"The axe of his death,
your beloved young priest,
will sink in your breast."

Three little sisters
dark on the bright moor,
hearing the doves' knell.
The name of the sun
was Maria; the name
of the moon, Isabel.

Una Noche Oscura

Salí sin ser notada . . .
Mi casa ya estando sosegada. *
St. John of the Cross

I went out without being noticed.
I had become the door, the courtyard,
the orchard, the path.

My house being now at rest.
Resting the hearth on my shoulder,
rocking the bed in my hand.

I went out without being noticed.
I had become the trees, the blossoms,
the fragrance, the air.

My house being now at rest.
My mother, her mother, her mother's mother
wrapped up in my shawl.

I went out without being noticed.
I had become the sky, the blackness,
the ladder, the stars.

My house being now at rest.
My mother's mother
kissed her daughter.

Her mother's mother kissed hers.
Mother (my mother!) kissed me.
We went out without being noticed.

Changed by our holy
and natural communion,

Una Noche Oscura: A Dark Night.

*I went out without being noticed . . . my house being
now at rest.

26

the ladder became
a winged little girl.

She slipped underneath us
and bore up us all—
women and orchard and door
path and courtyard and shawl—

as fast as a lizard
climbing a wall.

And only this poem
flutters back
to tell of it.

Tout Me Dit

Light tells me
Peaks tell me
Sea tells me

Rain tells me
Trees tell me
Night tells me

Dawn tells me
Bells tell me
Prayer tells me

Heat tells me
Clouds tell me
Air tells me

Grain tells me
Birds tell me
Song tells me

Smoke tells me
Fields tell me
Dung tells me

Hay tells me
Stalls tell me
Milk tells me

Hair tells me
Toes tell me
Breath tells me

Tout Me Dit: Every-
thing tells me.

Thread tells me
Bows tell me
Silk tells me

Bed tells me
Pots tell me
Soap tells me

Rust tells me
Cracks tell me
Death tells me

Hope tells me too
But words
Never do.

Monet's Cliff at Étretat

Moment to moment
I soften.

The worms
of water and air
draw near.

Fire is only a memory.

And earth,
the longed-for,
won't come now,

although I have smelled her
thousands of years.

Orantes

It has been a long time now
since clouds
touched us

Once in New York
on a cliff above the Hudson
a cloud
smiled down at me

A wide, sweet smile
that also embraced
the Cloisters

and may have been
drawn out by them

their wall-less walls
of stone
their pillowy roof tiles

where clouds
rested their breasts for
hundreds of years.

It has been a long time now
since clouds
touched us

relied on us to hold them
with hands upraised
and open

Orantes: people praying with raised arms
and open hands.

Rain

To plummet like stone
from a mountain of cloud
and hurt nothing

To fall over everything there is,
unhurt

To enter the earth without knocking

To be drunk by the mouths of trees,
swallowed by trunks
and come out unchanged
in the leaves

To be drawn
back up the mountain
on air-lifts

My Will

Can be a monstrance:
showing what is
become Who is

Or a gutter:
His body is left for dogs
and a voice excuses it,
"Dogs eat too."

Or sometimes:
the unseen farmer
growing the Unseen
wheat

Or purely saliva

A Continuation of the Fourteenth Elegy of Francis Jammes

—Le bel Été finit, me dis-tu.—C'est l'Automne,
Repondis-je. Et nos mots n'étaient plus si pareils. *

One day you will say to me, "I love her."
And I will say, "I am alone." And we will both
mean the same as we have always meant the same,
but we will forget that.
         In the deafening jazz
of the blood, I will think, "I am jealous." And
you will think, "I am guilty." But we will both
mean the same, "It is winter and relentless."

*The beautiful Summer is finished, you say to me. It is Autumn,
I answer. And our words are no longer so alike.

Losses

vivant de seule vie moite
enjoué avec les pierres et les feuillages*
André Frenaud

1.

Left and alone,
I don't even have these to play with:
leaves and stones and vodka.
All that I have is books
and O
how they can bark and bite me
and drag me to old abysses.
(Except for yours,
dear Agatha Christie.
What homage can repay you?)

2.

Need, wild Need—
I am still here,
your old worn fetus,
ticking inside you,
wound in your strings.
When I lie down,
I lie down in you.
Sans nom maintenant, sans visage
but O
how big and sharp your womb is,
mother of sorrows,
mad, mad Need.

*Living a lonely, wet life playing with stones
and foliage.

Sans nom maintenant, sans visage: without name
now, without face.

FOUR POEMS FOR MARIE LUISE KASCHNITZ

A Story

*Eine kleine Wendung, noch eine . . .**

A quarter-turn, two quarters, three
and suddenly: dryness and absence.
Dry skin, dry hair, dry nails,
dry friends, dry husband.
The water in all of us
fleeing through air.

Day after day
my skin and hair and nails
thirst for their water.
Nothing will do but this—
they fly off to find it,
dragging me after,
thirsty like them but fearful.
Up, up, up.

The wind in my face
is quick to tell me,
"I wouldn't look down in your place."
Nevertheless, I do, and pick out my Jane.
She is way, way below me
but her shoes are no longer in water.
They are over the water
walking on air.

Staring back up
I strain and I strain
to be able to tell her
how I see far off
like a vision glimpsed over mountains

*One small turn, then another.

36

that heavenly lake
where the streams of our bodies
drawn into clouds
pelt down as rain.

I want to call, "Jane!
God's blessing His holy waters.
If you squint, you'll see this—
the husks of the people above us
settling in drifts on the shore.
Now watch how He blows them,
how they waft to the water,
float a little, sink, and then
spring out on the far side
fresher than wet green stems."

The Poet Is Finally Admitted to the Hospital

Leuchtet der namenlose
*Unvergängliche Tempel**

Once upon a time
I stretched myself out
on the steps of the temple,
hurting but patient,
recovering, alone.
Faithful as doves,
the stars came out to show me
there is reliable beauty.
Night cupped its hand to my ear.
The moon turned her face
to smile on the columns,
stroking my eyes
with her white-gold finger.
The portal said over and over,
          "Come."
These were my mother and father.

But now
a torrent of crowds and voices
is pushing me into a wheel of questions,
rising and falling,
rising and falling,
always around and around.
Instead of the stars
are clowns who come at nightfall,
dressed up in grins and flowers.

*The nameless eternal temple shines.

The fierce roller coaster
of We-Know-Best
hurtles through 24 hours.
And worst of all
but hardly to be spoken of:
the terrible, lying mirrors.

No one
except a discredited patient
is singing a song
of the afterlife.
No one is planting the lilies
that perfume the soul.
No one is asking me,
"Swallow this capsule of trust,
dear Lynn.
It will do all it can do for you,
until we are able to bring you
the Bread of Life
and wine."

Other

Und draussen das flirrende Laub
*Das deinen Atem nicht braucht**

I am trying
to coax my attention
away from my soul.
It's the soul's whistle
she always listens for,
the soul's sticks
she brings back panting.

I want her to play
in my eyes' front yard.
I want her to go
on a run with my eyes,
free of her lead,
slipping her collar.

Pay attention,
Attention.
I am sending you off
on a long vacation.
Go roll in the sand,
nose under boulders,
leap up a trail
through poppies and lupine.

See! Here is our soul
coming to bundle you
into the train,

*And outside are the whirling leaves which do
not need your breath.

waving goodby,
and calling—
because she *is* the soul
and has to think of Later—

"Please bring me back
a fresh, natural tonic:

"The sight of tall pine trees
bent back in half
and licked by the seawind,

"Or an offshore rock
like a cupcake
baked by a giant
and patchily frosted with gulls,

"Or a mountain whose peak
of mile-high snow
hits you like a fist
straight in your words
and knocks them out for hours.

"I want this for my youngest—Age—
when she matures and needs it."

Ordination

Vorweggenommen in ein Haus aus Licht*

They always ask him
how he can give up
sweet, rounded breasts,
the tenderest fruit
on the tree of Carnal Knowledge,
long, slender fingers,
each one a harpist
with skin and muscle,
and the Cave of the Mysteries
where men are all changed
into Circean angels
who grunt as they soar.

He doesn't know
how he gives those up.
He knows they don't give him up.
They parade at nighttime
across his body,
a leering company
of unholy ghosts.
Like a hundred two-legged chocolates,
they draw near his mouth
and jump back when he opens it.

But dawn wakes him safely.
She sings to him, "Adam,
I am your call to come home,
home to the altar of Eden,
guarded by pure white angels
whose wings are tucked into beeswax
like swords in sheaths,
whose faces are fiery *Fiats*.
Here God has ordained

*From the beginning in a house of light.

no nose is equal to the fragrance,
no eyes to the beauty,
no ears to the love noise.

His senses fall from him
like old dead tissue.
God softly enters his fresh,
bare soul, stroking its knot
of nerves until they shiver.
He leaves its womb
filled up and breathing.
In time He delivers it
of that new life, matures it.

Day after day,
the priest will carry
his soul's small daughter
until she grows,
holds him for support
and then supports him.
She will bear him,
day after day,
until he withers.
In time she will lay him
to rest on her pallet,
smooth his harsh breath.

She will slip him
through the death canal
and wait for him on That Side,
her breast uncovered.
Her milk will run over his lips
while men who let their souls die childless
will put out their tongues
weakly, over and over,
hoping to lick up the dust from the air
and feed themselves with it.

The Voices of Time

FOR SAPPHO, A LIBATION

She who tastes the grape
feels the power of the god within her,
but she who sips the juice of your mouth,
                    Sappho,
is powerless.

> I do not like even the poems I wrote
> for you, Myrtho.

Blow your trumpet, Triton,
   for little Hero, of three summers' length,
has conquered your tumbling waters.

> The third spring, Gongula . . .

> Forget, Aphrodite, that you were born
> from the retreating wave.

You crushed the virgin in me, Sappho.

To Anaktoria and Atthis

We have unsalted the sea
      and bred the thornless rose,
we three.

> I would admit even the Muse
> while I feared for your safety, Atthis.

Oldest of all beloved beings:
    the stars.

                Memory, gather your daughters around me.

To Rhoda

This rose is shyer than a violet.

                    Your breasts are not small, Mnasdika;
                        they balance your slender body.

Your body is a foreign place, Gyrinno,
    its ports full of strangers.

The curve of your lip maddens me.

                    Night is kinder than Dawn and
                        your husband.

For Her Daughter

Learn archery, Kleis, or gardening,
    not poetry or love.

                    Lysander, you are as silent
                        as an unfinished god

Do not speak to Alkaios, Muse.
        Come, sit by me.

                    When I go to the house of Hades,
                        I will not leave you, Muses.

Her Last Summer

This light puts out my eyes.
        Kleis, your arm . . .

To the Moon

                    I am walking into the sea to find you.

Glykera Leaves the School of Sappho

My lover's breasts
are more beautiful than waves.

(In truth, I do not know
what it is she desires of me.)

She lifts her face like a violet
when my eyes brighten.

She curves her head to my breast.
the flickering of her tongue . . .

Sweetness and sweetness.

Can I play upon you, Leukonoe,
with a ghostly organ?

My lips tighten.
How they long to be given free rein,

to gallop over the hard country.

I will sink to my death
in this softness.

The Warrior Goddess
in Her Elements

Heavy in the hunting season,
pleased with their joint kill,
toasting their skill.

Air prepared them, blew off
exhalations of the chase.

With kindling hands,
they fed each other's fire.

Wet, lustrous.
Each one the shell
and the sea-roar.

Eve and Adam

Kains Augen sind nicht gottwohlgefällig*

They will not go, they will not go.
They cling to the waist of a tamarind tree

and crouch down low, beseeching,
"Leave this to us. To our children."

At that last word their spirits darken.

The Knowledge has opened their inner eyes.
They see the souls of their first-born sons

curled up at each side of Eve's soul,
fleshless for now and drowsing.

They know it will take a garden of angels,
exuding God's grace like myrrh and balsam,

and God Himself strolling through Eden,
instructing both them and the angels,

to cure their Cain.

*Cain's eyes are not pleasing to God.

The Deserted Wife

Und Hagar und ihr Knablein sanken in
das gelbe Fell*
Else Lasker-Schuler

Once I thought I was Sarah.
Now I see I am Hagar.

Once my son's name was Isaac.
Now Ishmael is his dusty name.

Ish-ma-el: three small tracks in the desert
where tears are the only footprints.

Perhaps there was never a Sarah.

Perhaps there was never a shower of angels
making my womb an oasis.

Perhaps there was always only Sarai.
Abraham too could be a mirage.

I would think that, I would, except
I hear how Ishmael cries in the night for him.

*And Hagar and her young boy sank into the yellow skin.

The Death of Moses

*Sein Lächeln grüsste den ersehnten Heimatstern**

Israel's elders are watching over Moses.

His ears have become like old sea lions
that twitch in their sleep at storms on the water.

He dreams that the waves are acclaim for the hero,
the wild young man he himself has anointed.

And Joshua suddenly strides among the people,
fresh from the tent where he has prayed, unsleeping.

A star appears on the warrior's forehead.
It detaches itself and glides into the heavens.

Moses alone sees nothing of the miracle.
Age has turned his eyes into gumtrees.

Israel's eyes are like golden idols
that shine in the light of Joshua's splendor.

The power of God leads the new star higher,
to the last degree but one of its position.

The star stops there. It waits. And waits.
. . . .

The people of Israel murmur in confusion.
Joshua's sun-baked skin turns pale.

*His smile greeted the longed-for homeland-star.

The elders kneeling by Moses shiver.
They leave his pallet and stare into the heavens,

at the Almost-covenant,
which holds their hopes in its shining fingers.

Moses unsheltered grows cold and stiffens.
The star leaps down as his last breath leaves him.

It catches that breath and drinks of it deeply.
God leads it back up, enthrones it over Canaan.

Esther

*Der König lächelt ihrem Nahen entgegen**

Her heart has broken God's second law.
It bears a golden image on its altar.

When the king calls, "Esther,"
Mordecai's image reddens like a furnace.

Esther delivers her flesh to the king
as an olive is laid in the oil press.

Within the queen's soul is her uncle's niece,
who hides herself behind a veil of meekness.

She lowers her gaze when the queen looks up,
at royal command, to the Royal Eyes.

She cannot not remember how the Eyes
had gazed at the statue Vashti

and found it full of living grace,
how they see nothing strange in Haman's face.

*The king smiles her near to him.

Joseph

Zehn Wölfe gingen an meine Tränke*

They told me I had a tower.
I knew that I had a well.

My brother's towers despised me.
They threw me into a well.

(My father always suspected.
He guessed at *his* father's well.)

Potiphar's wife was mistaken.
She believed that she had a well.

She wanted the tower she thought I had.
I covered my well and fled.

When Pharoah appeared, I opened.
He fell full-length to my depth.

I swallowed him and exulted.
We pledged a great pledge and kept it:

Keep this secret from God.

*Ten wolves went to my trough.

Jacob and Esau

Rebekkas Magd ist eine himmlische Fremde*

They ate the roses, drank the light
Rebecca's heavenly maid had made them.

So this day came:
they were gold and fragrant.

The friends of Esau
rode off to hunt without him.

Their horses tossed their manes and snorted,
"Esau is a faggot."

Esau spit out the roses
and vomited up the light.

Jacob's friends paraded past him,
holding their noses.

"Jacob is a sissy."
"Jacob is a mama's boy."

He stood at first like a burdened ass,
then shook like a tethered kid,

and then—

darted out, head down, and caught them,
knocking them all to the ground.

*Rebecca's maid is a heavenly stranger.

He showered their dusty hair with petals,
braying and splitting his sides.

After he lay on the cool tent floor
to cure the pain in his forehead.

He slept till his cousin the moon woke up,

then slipped away from his parents' watch
and ran to a shrine in the hills.

There at the back of an ancient stone
he opened his shepherd's wallet,

took out two sandwiches of roses,
a wineskin of light.

Gottschalk, Alone in His Heresy,
After Years of Forced Enclosure,
Begs His Friend, Walafrid Strabo,
to Aid Him When Death Comes, AD 845

Nothing flowers in my spirit.
Earth and rain are needed there.
All I am is hearth and kindling.
Walafrid, I ask your prayer.

Why your God brought me to Fulda,
why Hrabanus bound me here,
nothing bends itself to answer.
All I learn is harsh and sere.

You who tend your herbal garden,
fresh each dawn with glistening dew,
know what happens if the Sun-cart
wheels too near the mint and rue.

When the bishops close their circle,
when the burning vengeance comes,
Walafrid, leave your grassy studies.
Close my eyes with your green thumbs.

Hrabanus Maurus, Dying,
Confesses His Kinship
with Gottschalk in an
Unsent Letter of Love, AD 856

Burning reeds are burning brands
that fire homes and barns.
I had to stamp on your thin grass
or you would do more harm.

But what I grieve for on this bed
is *vanitas*, my pride,
that made me slam your open door
and caged you in my side.

I was the rood on which you hung
as child, as youth, as man.
This wood is rotting now, my son;
it has outlived its span.

I want to tell you how at court
I bore, like you, a weight.
In Fulda and both times in Mainz
I leaned toward faith in Fate.

I almost shouted, "I am damned.
There is no ground for hope."
I saved my soul by lashing it
to God with Paul's strong rope.

We two have heard the siren's song,
her voice so soft and loud.

So when I rest on Lazarus' breast,
I'll reach down through the cloud

And pour sweet draughts of water
to cool your life-long hell.
For you are not the rich man
and God's a depthless well.

Hroswitha of Gandesheim

Nothing
drew me out
of myself
at an early age.
I stayed
at the roots
of my being
and there
I flourished,
playing the pipes
of Pan.
My breath
is the breathing
of Him
Who made me.
My mind is
perpetual
spring.

An Old Monk
of St. Benigny

Over the earth
the *vagantes* go,
feasting at midnight,
sleeping in sun,
playing with laps
and with meters.

Arthritis
and the abbot
are keeping
me here.

I feel the horizons.

They shuffle
and turn in the night.
When I put out
my hand, they
bark me away.

Vagantes: wandering monks.

Notker Balbulus
Hears the Confession
of a Young Monk of St. Gall

As though
passion
were a tide
washing up
from a source
that is wilder
than Ireland,
"I have never
gone down
to the shore,"
he cried.

The Escape of Our Beloved Father,
St. John of the Cross, in the Octave
of the Assumption, August 1578

His hands are busily
knotting the blankets,
testing the roof-beam.
God sends the moon
to illuminate and guide him
to this one end:
a dish of baked pears.

Dropping six feet
to the shore of the Tagus,
he awakens the rocks.
They all jump up, barking
and snapping at air.
He beseeches the moon
to quiet them and pet them.
She soothes them
with one gold finger.

Surrounded by walls,
he half-falls in a swoon.
How can he pick himself up
in his arms as a father
would carry a daughter?
Can anyone haul up
the earth to the moon?
He thanks his shod brothers
who lightened his load
by a quarter.

He prays to the Moon
of the Church
who leans out from her

twelve stars to hear him.
With one silver *Ave*
she vaults him cleanly
up the city wall.

He jumps to the street
where a sweet-faced woman,
the moon of the drinkers
who come to her inn,
invites him to stay.
"I cannot do that,
my child," he smiles.

He takes the wrong turn
at the *Zocodover*,
missing St. Joseph's,
its windows still shining
with light from those moons,
the eyes of St. Teresa
("The soul is a castle
of one big diamond").

He encounters a servant.
"May I stay until dawn,
rolled up in the porch
of your master's fine home,
like a beggarly star
at the foot of the moon?"
The servant allows him.

He leaves in the morning
and finds his way back
to the Carmelite convent.
He knocks on the half-
moon door of the turn.
Leonore of Jesus admits him.

The prioress, Anna
of the Angels, thanks God.
She claps her old hands

and says to the Sisters,
"We are like sailors
who let down their nets
to catch a few cod
and bring up the light-
brimming moon."

St. John cannot answer.
His words are eclipsed
by that hot sun, Wrong.
The Leo of his steps
has changed into Cancer.
Teresa of the Conception
brings him baked pears.
The pears bear him tears
and the tears bear him song.

"In the beginning
was only the Light,
a three-folded Light.
One of the Folds
did not cling to the Light
but emptied Himself
and turned into Night.

"It is Night from Whose breasts
we suck our sweet rest,
Who cradles our limbs
for a third of our life;
it is Night Who miscarries
our sin and our strife.

"The Light and the Night
together made Sight.
Women and men had been
blind until Night
sent forth Their vision
to fill up their sight—"

And then he put down
the pen of his voice
as Night caught him up
to give him new sight
in darkness.

Rejoice.

Complaint

*Ronsard avant moi et Baudelaire ont
chanté le regret des vieilles . . .**
Robert Desnos

What can they know of regrets
of old women—Ronsard, Baudelaire
who abandoned old breasts
to conventional darkness,
who just didn't see: thin hair,
sunk cheeks, slackened muscles,
who looked in dim eyes
for a moment to say,
"Marie, Marie, did I know you?"
And then to the servant of lust
who always waits in the doorway,
"Bring me Elise,
whose breasts are as tender as grapes
and throw out this mouldy vine."

(Marie, who still had the circus
of love within her, savaged the wire
of the tightrope dancer, snapped off
trapezes, threw the ringmistress
out of the tent, ripped up the guy-ropes,
and flayed the blind elephants:
"Lay die and die, you ugly gray hulks.
Feed on starvation. You disgust even me.")

*Ronsard before me and Baudelaire have sung of the
regret of old women.

Cities

The culture that you love
I also seek to touch.
So light gathers in our eyes
when the sun rises
over a piece of incarnate time
that angels of the mind support
(and demons tortured bodies for).

We honor the ghost of Rome.
We honor her blood too
where it flows in the veins
of her northern descendants,
our great port-cities of the word trade.

I haunt the galleries
of Manhattan, empty the library
shelves, fill up my ears
with the words of living poets,
and dedicate my senses
to the urban Muse
whose shrines are as numerous as Venus's.

But the curtains of my apartment
are stiff with soot; there's
a sour smell and drifts of dust
on the bookcase. The bad breath
of cities.
        We say we love these
and yet they are cruel to us.

Cruel are the foxes of the city.
Oppressive its pigs.
And dangerous the thoroughbreds
racing the city's courses,
whose hoofs, at a glance,
could knock us brainless.

Rosa Kaufman-Pasternak

Of course her son would give up
music. How could he continue,
first riding the tide of her passion,
and then be borne aloft
in fire like Elias when a greater
than he was barred?

For she to whom he was devoted
had seen her genius torn from her hands,
had lost it to the old pogróm,
that Russo-Oriental strangulation
of the soul, aimed at outstanding
female serfs, daughters of boyars,
tsarevnas.

Deep in her heart, the decades brought
wave after wave of powerful harmonies,
like barges washing up to be unloaded.
Rosa, to whom they had belonged since childhood,
was pushed like a child away
from the river.

The decree had been set:
"It is not for you to read
the bills of lading, it is not
for you to strain at heavy labor,
to give out treasure,
to ennoble Russia and your century."

Rosa Kaufman-Pasternak (1867–1939) was the mother of Boris
Pasternak. She experienced "the impossibility of combining
the dazzling career of a brilliant concert pianist with the busy life
of a solicitous, self-effacing wife and anxious mother" (Lydia
Pasternak).

Vladimir Mayakovsky Defends Rosa Pasternak

C'mon! Give her the bloody piano!
What will it cost you?

Gentlemen of the chamber,
we're all true Soviets here:

Give her the bloody piano.

You won't have to open
your wallets again.

She can eat a piano
and wear a piano

and sleep on the keys.

Comrade gentlemen,
you are holding her back

for her good, you say,
to protect her little fingers

from the snapping of pianos.

But some of us know,
although nobody hears you saying,

how fearful you are that Rosa,
in charge of her own piano,

will ride it like a tank

right through your ears
and into your brain.

And for all your king's horses
and all your king's men

you won't be the same!

Dino Campana and His Servitors, 1932

The staff of the madhouse
is clocking in. "The sun is hot
already." "Baskets and baskets
of squash I got, all of them
big but tender like veal."
"The smell of these roses could
knock you down." "Hell, a wasp!"
They throw up the windows
on overgrown lawns, on bushes
so thick that the paths are smothered.

Dino stands in the mud of his room
and wrings out his sodden shirt.
He watches the chilly water
run down his fingers
and more pour out of the sky.
He sees how a small tornado
is lifting the whole asylum,
how all of them hurtle
straight toward the walls
and the walls blow out and flee them.

Dino Campana, an Italian poet (1881–1932), was
hospitalized permanently for insanity in 1918.

Josefina Manresa Admonishes Her Fiancé Miguel Hernandez

Miguel,
see me.
Look
with the
wide-open
eyes
of your heart,
and not
with the
small red
squint
of your
penis,
hysterical
and fat
with tears.

Sacred and Profane Secrets: The Brontë Poems

Mrs. Brontë Finds Her Page in the Gospels, September 1821

A smile can be as true as a wound
but the smile has shrunk
and the wound has grown.
A soldier of Herod has forced in the door.
It isn't a child struck down by his sword.

Cries will rise to the sky very soon,
the cries of children
who moan for their home.
Rachel will comfort their tears no more.
She prays they may be restored by the Word.

Maria Branwell Brontë (1782-1821).

Maria Lives and Dies in Two Testaments, May 1825

First-born of the father,
playing before him,
lighting his eyes.

I am the mother
of fair love and knowledge,
I am the mother of hope.

I stood at my station
beneath life's cross
until the day came

To climb it.
After my body is taken down,
Resurgam.

Maria Brontë (1813–1825).

Resurgam: I shall rise.

Ain Karim Comes to Elizabeth, June 1825

The years of grace,
a decade.

One joyful mystery:
Fiat!

And then—
a Visitation.

My soul leaps
at its greeting,

does not come down.

Elizabeth Brontë (1814–24).

Ain Karim: A Judean town,
site of the Visitation (Luke
1:39–44).

Fiat: let it be.

Aunt Branwell Is Unchanged by Death, October 1842

Leaving the bright
gardens of Cornwall,

Leaving its mild
sea air, its houses

Full of soft light
and friendships,

I came to this scouring
land, where winds bend back

The two or three trees
and the ground swells up

in colors the color
of bruises: green

and brown and purple.

I knew my duty.
It lay uphill.

My nieces have done me credit.
My nephew? Well . . .

In Cornwall
we all saw treasure sink

And ships break up
that bore it.

Aunt Branwell, Maria Branwell Brontë's
sister (1780–1842).

Branwell Wishes He Could Say
Like Hannah, "I Have Drunk Neither Wine Nor Strong Drink," September 1847

What I made in my image,
poem and painting,
I could not sell.

God and my father
understood that well.
Both had had problems
with marketing art.

But God is a master
at laboring hard
without ever stopping
or giving up heart.

And my father had mastered
the stopping part.

My Father and my father
for thirty-one years
called me and called me
without one lull,

"Branwell, Samuel,
Branwell, Samuel."

I shook at the summons
but would not wake up,

Branwell Brontë (1817–47).

pulled down my nightcap
over my ears,

Said to the Voices,
"I am not here,"
and drowned my fear
at the Bull.

Death Too Is Life to Emily, December 1847

These winter winds,
your heather,
the triune sun
we saw together
sang to me
in their glory,

"Before the daystar,
like the dew,
we have begotten you."
There is only one life,
one story.

Heathcliff and Branwell
and Anne
are a hawk and a hound
and a spaniel.

Hero and Keeper and Flossy
are queens of the south.

The moors in the moonlight
can rival great
Solomon's temple.

The birth of a verse
is as sweet as
the Shulamith's mouth.

Emily Jane Brontë (1818–48).

Hero, Keeper, Flossy: Brontë family pets.

Anne Discloses the Secret of Her Peace, May 1848

Whatever connects
God's world to this
runs through me.

Even exhausted
by four great griefs
I feel it:

a Something
stretched under
flesh and air.

My hands let go.
My feet balance themselves
on prayer.

Hour by hour
this soft sweet May,
I slip through
the open doorway.

Anne Brontë (1819–48).

Charlotte's Last Letter to Ellen Nussey, March 1855

You can hide among rocks
in the rifts of the crag

or bury in dust
this face which doomed me.

Moons, sabbaths, assemblies,
I hate them with all my heart.

The way of the self-deceived
is bitter. Last night I prayed,

"O God, draw back my life
ten months as You drew back

the shadow on Ahaz' sundial."
His word in my womb told me today,

"You did not love
what He gave You first,

when you lived alone,
were fruitful."

This singer of songs
will not rise up.

Boil no more figs
for a plaister.

Charlotte Brontë (1816–55); Ellen Nussey, Char-
lotte's lifelong friend.

St. Jerome Looks with
Fellow-Feeling at the Reverend Patrick Brontë in His Study, April 1855

A family translated
to books and skulls:

All that live here
are the word and the pen.

And out there—
barren and arrogant men.

I know what heart
he will find in them!

Women alone
took and reproduced us.

Rev. Patrick Brontë (1777–1861).

Lynn Butler, a native of New York City, is a writer, editor, coun-
selor, and college English instructor. She is a graduate of the
College of Mount St. Vincent and New York University. Her
poems have won first prize in the Florida Poetry Contest and
have appeared in *The Raddle Moon, The Crescent Review, Kalliope,*
and *The Florida Review.* In 1982 she was a James Dickey Fellow at
the Atlantic Center for the Arts. She lives with her husband,
Gerald J. Schiffhorst, in Winter Park, Florida.